Big sea animals

Come and look

at the fish.

The fish is big.

3

Come and look

at the crocodile.

The crocodile is big.

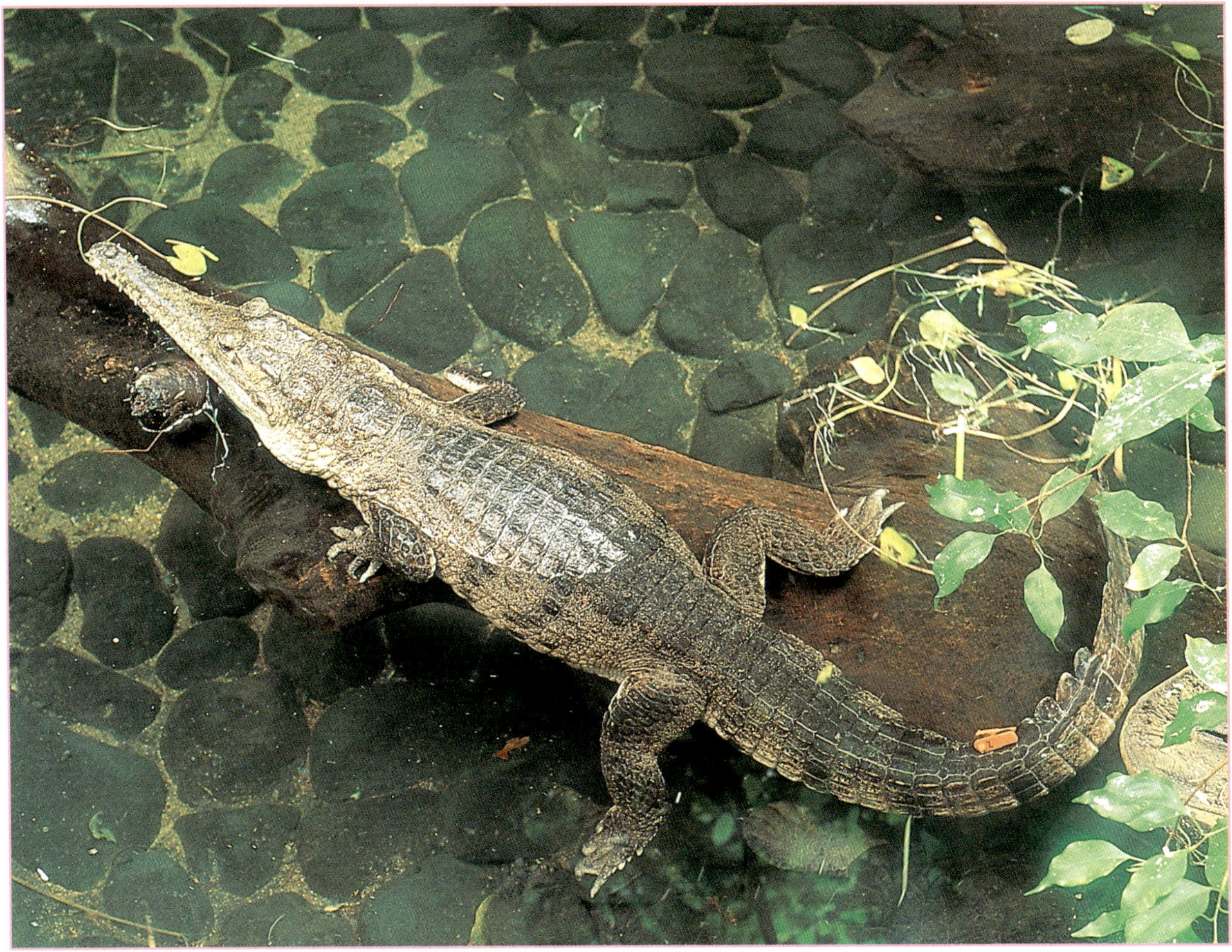

Come and look

at the turtle.

The turtle is big.

7

Come and look

at the dolphin.

The dolphin is big.

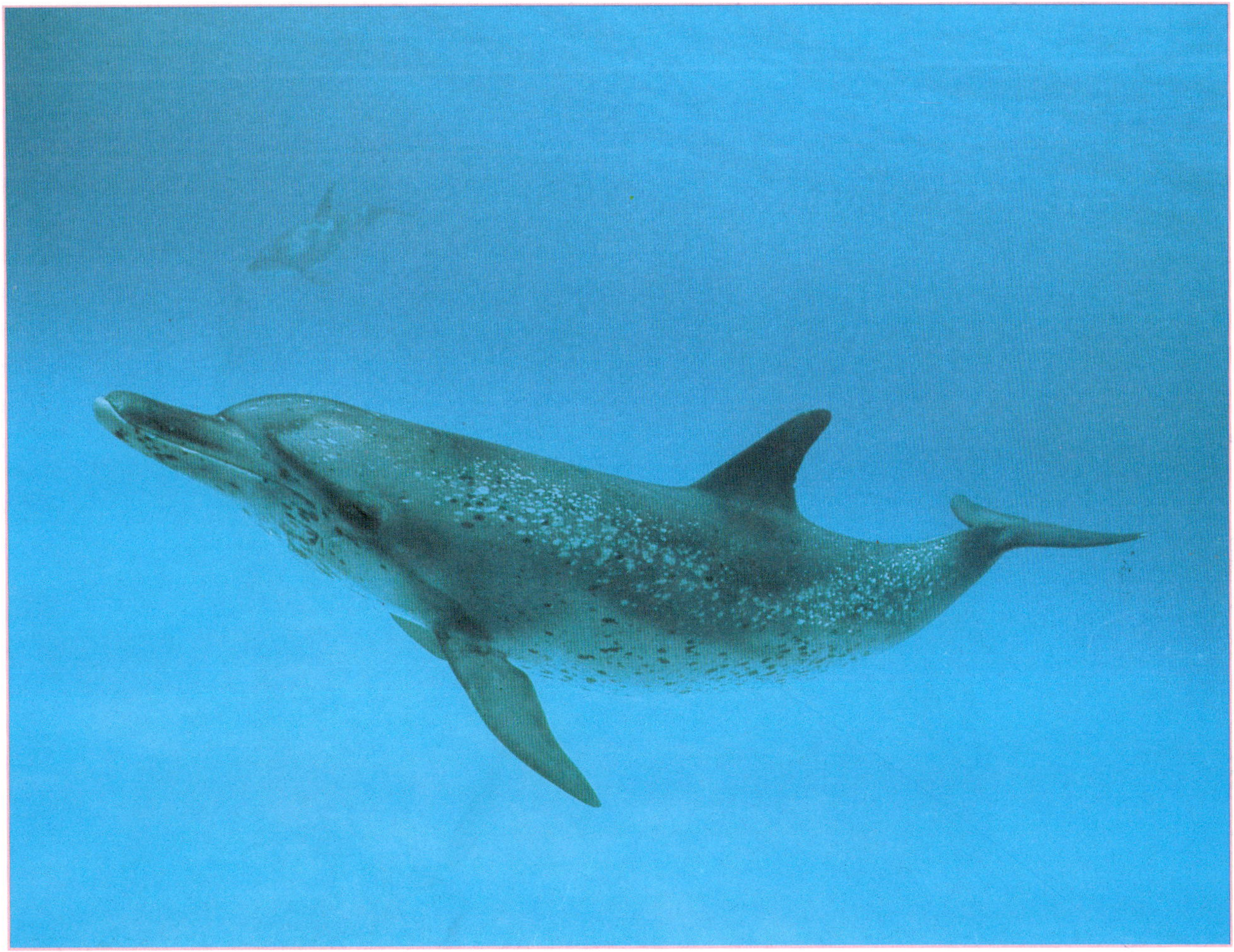

Come and look

at the sting-ray.

The sting-ray is big.

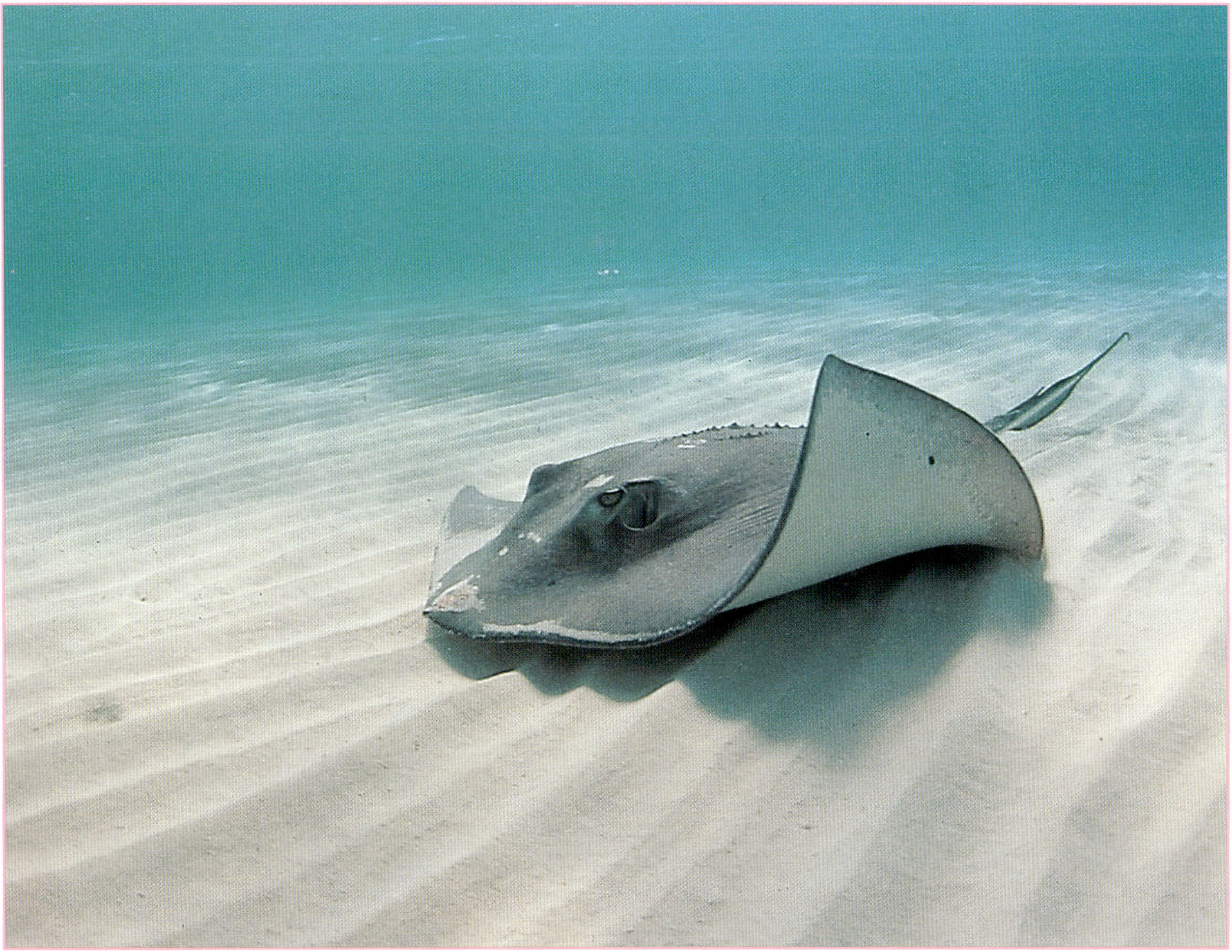

Come and look

at the octopus.

The octopus is big.

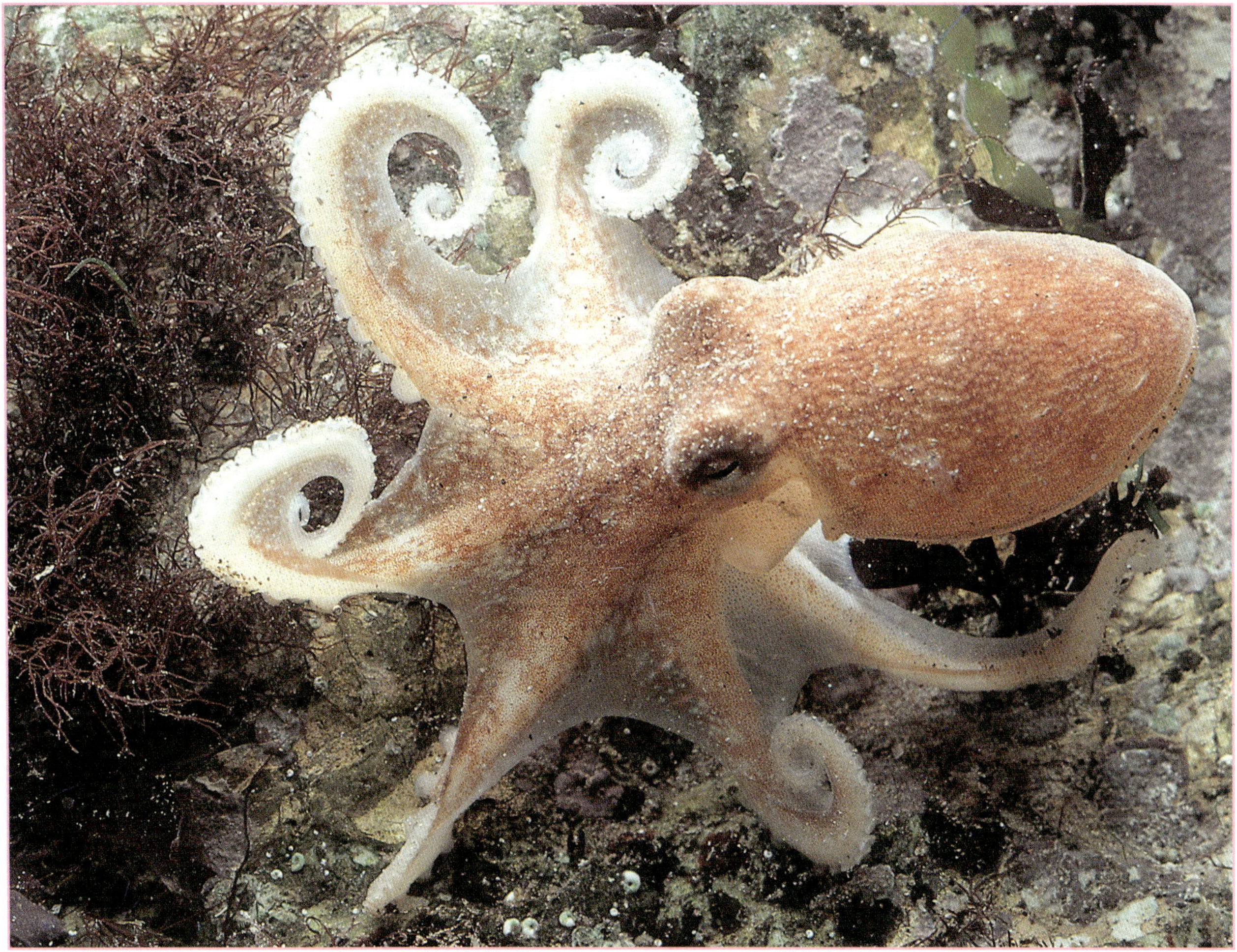

Come and look

at the sea lion.

The sea lion is big.

Look at the big shark.